The U.S. Armed Forces

The U.S. Army Special Operations

by Angie Peterson Kaelberer

Reading Consultant:
Barbara J. Fox
Reading Specialist
North Carolina State University

Capstone
press

Mankato, Minnesota

Blazers is published by Capstone Press,
151 Good Counsel Drive, P.O. Box 669, Mankato, Minnesota 56002.
www.capstonepress.com

Library of Congress Cataloging-in-Publication Data
Kaelberer, Angie Peterson.
The U.S. Army Special Operations / by Angie Peterson Kaelberer.
    p. cm.—(Blazers. The U.S. Armed Forces)
    Includes bibliographical references and index.
    ISBN 0-7368-3795-7 (hardcover)
    1. Special forces (Military science)—United States—Juvenile literature.
2. United States. Army—Juvenile literature. I. Title. II. Series.
UA34.S64K34 2005
356'.16'0973—dc22   2004018312

Summary: Describes the missions, weapons, and equipment of the U.S. Army
Special Operations.

Credits
Juliette Peters, set designer; Enoch Peterson and Steve Christensen,
    book designers; Jo Miller, photo researcher; Scott Thoms, photo editor

Photo Credits
AP/Wide World Photos/Brennan Linsley, 27
Corbis/Annie Griffiths Belt, 15; Reuters, 19, 21 (bottom); SYGMA/Patrick
    Durand, 11
Corel, cover (background)
DVIC/Michael Lemke, 14
Getty Images Inc./Erik S. Lesser, 13 (top); Staff Sgt. Cherie A. Thurlby, USAF,
    21 (top); Time Life Pictures/Steve Liss, 22
Photo by Ted Carlson/Fotodynamics, cover (helicopter), 13 (bottom), 16–17,
    20, 23, 25, 28–29
U.S. Army/Nancy Fischer, 6, 7, 9 (both); SSG Amanda C. Glenn, 5, 8, 12
William B. Folsom, cover (soldier)

**Capstone Press thanks Walter Sokalski Jr., Deputy Public Affairs Officer,
U.S. Army Special Operations Command, Fort Bragg, North Carolina, for
his assistance with this book.**

1 2 3 4 5 6 10 09 08 07 06 05

Table of Contents

Special Operations in Action

Army Special Operations Rangers drop from a Black Hawk helicopter. The Rangers are on a rescue mission.

MH-60 Black Hawk

★★★★★★★★★★★★★★★

5

One Ranger stays on the roof. He guards the other Rangers as they climb to the ground. On the ground, another Ranger aims his M-249 weapon.

Carl Gustov antitank weapon

M-249 weapon

BLAZER FACT

By law, only men can attend the Special Forces Qualification Course or Ranger School.

Ranger Special
Operations Vehicle

MH-47 Chinook
helicopter

More Rangers arrive. They help
rescue captured soldiers. When the
mission is over, the Black Hawk picks up
the Rangers. They return to their post.

Missions

The Army calls Special
Operations units "Special Ops."
The Special Ops soldiers
perform dangerous missions.

Green Berets

Special Ops includes different groups. Green Berets lead surprise attacks. Rangers do rescues and make airfields safe. Night Stalkers often fly in darkness.

Army Rangers

Night Stalkers

13

Not all soldiers can serve in Special
Ops units. Soldiers go through weeks
of difficult tests and training. They work
hard to become Special Ops members.

Rescue training

BLAZER FACT

Each Special Forces
soldier can speak at
least one language
other than English.

M-134 Minigun

Power supply plug

Bullets

Bullet cartridges

Gunner

Weapons, Vehicles, and Equipment

Special Ops soldiers use Humvees to move from place to place. Guns are mounted on these vehicles.

Humvee

MH-47E Chinook helicopter

Special Ops soldiers travel in helicopters and airplanes. They jump into enemy territory. Parachutes help them land safely on the ground.

C-5 Galaxy airplane

Night scope

BLAZER FACT

The movie *Black Hawk Down* tells the story of Rangers who rescued U.S. soldiers in Somalia.

Night vision goggles and night scopes help soldiers see in the dark. Special Ops soldiers use ropes to drop into enemy territory from helicopters.

Special Ops Jobs

Special Ops members
have different jobs. Some are
engineers or pilots. Others
are medics or radio operators.

Special Ops units have both officers and enlisted members. Officers have more education and training. All Special Ops members help keep the United States safe.

ARMY RANKS

★ ★ ★ ★ ★ ★ ★ ★ ★ ★ ★ ★ ★ ★ ★ ★

ENLISTED	OFFICERS
Private	Lieutenant
Specialist	Captain
Corporal	Major
Sergeant	Colonel
	General

MH-6 Little Bird
helicopters

Glossary

enlisted member (en-LIST-id MEM-bur)—a member of the military who is not an officer

medic (MED-ik)—a soldier who is trained to give medical help

mission (MISH-uhn)—a military task

officer (OF-uh-sur)—a soldier who directs enlisted members in their duties

parachute (PAR-uh-shoot)—a large piece of strong, lightweight cloth; parachutes allow people to jump from high places and float safely to the ground.

weapon (WEP-un)—anything used when fighting; guns, tanks, and bombs are weapons.

Read More

Burgan, Michael. *U.S. Army Special Operations Forces: Airborne Rangers.* Warfare and Weapons. Mankato, Minn.: Capstone Press, 2000.

Cooper, Jason. *U.S. Special Operations.* Fighting Forces. Vero Beach, Fla.: Rourke, 2004.

Green, Michael, and Gladys Green. *The Green Berets at War.* On the Front Lines. Mankato, Minn.: Capstone Press, 2004.

Internet Sites

FactHound offers a safe, fun way to find Internet sites related to this book. All of the sites on FactHound have been researched by our staff.

Here's how:

1. Visit *www.facthound.com*
2. Type in this special code **0736837957** for age-appropriate sites. Or enter a search word related to this book for a more general search.
3. Click on the **Fetch It** button.

FactHound will fetch the best sites for you!

Index